GRANDMA'S ATTIC
MOM'S HDB
MY WALLPAPER

### Acknowledgements

*All my writing would not have been possible without God,
my parents, and the faith of my mentors Arthur Yap and
Edwin Thumboo. I thank the good people, too many to
name here, who bless me as friends, publishers, classmates,
colleagues and students.*

Published by
Landmark Books Pte Ltd
5001 Beach Road
#02-73/74
Singapore 199588

ISBN 978-981-18-0612-4

Printed by Oxford Graphic Printers Pte Ltd

# GRANDMA'S ATTIC
# MOM'S HDB
# MY WALLPAPER

Heng Siok Tian

⋄LANDMΛRK⋄BOOKS⋄

*In loving memory of my parents,*
*Teo Ah Lee and Heng Kin Chua.*

*With gratitude to Edwin Thumboo.*

# CONTENTS

## Open Coffin: Rainbow Blouse

A few Teochew phrases you left behind as oral memory
like beautiful bajus you stored away in the wardrobe;
teak wood that survived three house movings
like you enduring.

Kebayas you outgrew due to
age, burdens, extra weight,
your good taste in colours,
you kept them in pristine shape,
washed, ironed, crease-free:
hung in an order
(understood only by you).
Did you think for me
to burn them with you, to bring to your other home?

I imagine cremation fire brightening your way
only to be told by the undertakers
that a few pieces are now allowed in incineration,
only to be greeted by a sign at
Khong Meng San temple
that eco-burning is recommended,
and no more joss sticks.

Clothes did not show your deep shades.

Now,
each rainbow
reminds me of the rainbow striped blouse
you burned in.

## Grandma's Attic, Mom's HDB

At Lunar New Year's reunions,
my kid cousins and I would be banished
into grandma's attic to play hide and seek.

Once up there, there would be no coming down except
        to use the toilet or be whipped.
The women adults roasted in the kitchen preparing
        to feed an extended family.
Grandma would sit in the living room, fanning herself,

looking on as her four sons cracked at mahjong noisily,
half-nude (privilege of son-hood), swearing in singlets
while females were stewing near stoves.

We thought little of sanitation or hygiene.
Pickled food on open shelves tasted good.
A pot of braised meat was a special treat.

After food, it was back to the attic or a romp in the streets.
We replayed the scene till Grandma sold her Chinatown house
to buy each of her sons their HDBs.

After mother scrimped and saved for her first one-room flat,
I ran along common corridors. There were no daffodils
        near a brook.
I fell into a longkang.

I did not frolick among meadows; pastures; I smelled
        after-rain lallang.
I did not listen to nursery rhymes; pots and pans clanged constant.
I did not read the Bible (till much older); joss sticks burned my fears.

I did eat, sleep, shit (homely) enough in mom's HDB.
I did go to school,
picked up literacy, gained employability.

I prayed to gods, first my grandma's, then my mother's,
drank the water with ashes burnt from triangular yellow-paper
                    amulets.
Then I pray to my own.

## District 1: Tew Chew Street, 1930s

Make it
smell of ocean fish scales
make it
smudge with red of fresh gills
make it
sound like wet market din
make it
spread as a fish net grid
make it
taste as sea-water deep.

Make it sing
to market, to market
to buy a fat pig,
home again, home again
jiggety-jig.

Imagine that was mother's Tew Chew Street.

I want to give it a special smell of flooded drains
materialize it with humid human sweat skins
emboss it as a landmass
with paper textures resembling dirt roads and cart tracks
use Braille for place names.

I want it to sing
to market, to market
to sell a fresh fish,
home again, home again
rickety rich.

I want it to sing
in known and unknown dialects of our forefathers
hold it, smell it, hear it
as a
3D printed contour of District 1
for further mapping.

## Landing (8 Aug 2010)
## (Summer Course, Trinity Hall College, Cambridge, UK)

### (i) *Running away*

There's no running away
from parents,
even if you are 60 going on 61
and your parent 85 going on 86
even if you are presently parenting.

Father, mother, illiterate
took different jobs
at different times, different places
to feed us;
they only needed me to be in school,
to be a salaried worker.
They who never ever have been one
lived variously as hawkers, driver,
nanny, baby-sitter...

O mother, O father
O captain, my captain

They never knew school meant strange dreams
strolled into my rabbit head, made me speak strange Teochew,
acquired another tongue, with the moon-rabbit jumping
about in my dislocated globe.

There's no running away.
(I dreamt of it thirty years ago.)

Like any angry youth
(playthings of elizabethan gods,
when we now know better is but hormones)

I wanted running away to a cold island
having grown up in crammed rooms, with extended family,
in humidity, with sunshine and rain,
not having learnt the true meaning of damp cold,
visioning english classrooms,
bearded professors, distinguished colleges,
countryside and pastures,
rivers such as the thames and the cam
forgetting the waters at my feet –
myths of my own making.

Examine well the colour of my blood.

There's no running away.

Now I walk
on the side of the road along St Andrew's Street
with the Cambridge Magistrate Courts
and Grand Arcade Building
staring at me, estranged.
I looked back, different,
wandering along pavements,
in full view, The Lion Yard,
watching with eyes twenty years older,
Radley and Ted Baker
are on one side of the road,
my youth now inside me.

Salisbury, Tesco, Waitrose.

My heart is quaint again
remembering Yaohan, Magnolia Snack Bar,
Silver Spoon and red-brick National Library,
NTUC, Cold Storage, Sheng Siong..

What is it about a past
presenting its future?

## (ii) *Room among Ruins*

I walked by a door
labelled
Leslie Stephen's Room

I walked past green courtyards.
There were little ducks in tow sliding on folds
of a gently moving river.
I thought how picturesque the summer scene looked,
almost a live canvas in a gallery for pastoral past.

I think of you,
could not quite believe your learned father
too would privilege a boy's education to yours,
would now be less angry at my father who
too would value a son's education to a girl's.
Label it tradition (never mind Victorian, Chinese or unfair).

I walked by Grantchester,
into yet another bloomsy view of English tea sets,
leafy surroundings favoured by poets and writers.

I think of you,
could imagine how slow dying was for you in your room,
could not imagine what cold it was that drove you
to weigh stones in your robe as you waded out to a river
or put your head into an oven.
Label it madness (never mind inherited, stress-related or unfair).

I do not lead a parallel life to you.
even though we live in a parallel universe,
how to know when to let go and when to hold?

We are each a room framed in a museum in our globe.

## (iii) *Naming of a Child*

Chinese parents believe full well
how fates are sealed when they name their offsprings,
consulting zodiac signs, almanacs and ancestral spirits.
Surely it is not to colonize their child but to free them
to a future path of boundlessness.

Is there a comforting certainty
in an ordinary name, an everyday name
or a defiant, deflective will of belief
in calling their sons
a cow, a dog,
their daughters
ugly,
so that their fates will turn the exact opposite?

(I was told it was to lull the gods into complacency,
to think their child useless for their ends.)

The old wise, they share a wisdom I lack.

Naming is the first act of colonizing like planting a flag.

## Aftermath

### (i) *Unspoken love*

Red dust across the blue skies.
Time cares not our human sighs.

Mother risked her youth for her tomorrows,
Father won her with his handsomeness.

Both spurned the blessings of parents and heavens.
What prize passion? What gamble?

Am I the calm in their storm?
Are children the penance for defiance?

No one else remembers yesterday's lovers.
When one wakes from a dream, it's a dream.

He was her most exciting execution, costliest card.
She was his loveliest love, costliest cut.

### (ii) *Remembering Parents*

When people die, they become butterflies,
or so I thought many moons ago as a silly little girl.

When people die, they become ash,
they need little space in an urn as they grow large daily.

### *Recovery (i)*

After a parent's death
as you clean out the closets,
you might find
a 1964 receipt of her first HDB instalment,
creased pawnshop ticket,
foreign notes, old cold coins....

If you are lucky, you might find
a very small, old black-and-white photo of her own parents.

After my mother's death
I found all her
tenderness folded between clothes.

### *Recovery (ii)*

On life's stage
mothers and children, fathers and children
all must part, must depart.

On my stage
we are passing clouds whispering in a world
filled with unspoken hurts.

While listening to a concert,
I did not hear time's winged chariot swinging by,
did not notice your frail limbs as you danced on cue.

When the final curtain call comes,
the silence is mournful,
thaws my cold as water in my eyes.

Mother, I need to be half-awake, half asleep,
then at least in my dream, I could say in my seat
I miss you (always too late).

You are on a different stage.
I leave the theatre solo.

## Simple Days
### (Remembering Mother in Portugal, June 2015)

### *Day 1*

In a postcard on its way to you, it's an early summer.
Not knowing words, you will not read
my scribbles but you read people, faces;
eyes now cataract-cleansed
look past colours, surfaces,
nuances you shape well
with clarity of age.
Mother, how might I learn your wisdom? How?
How do you bear your pain?
Suffering the silence only mothers see
in darkness but
just now the light was good.

### *Day 2*

Summer light drives me inside a postcard café.
I carry your small photo with me on this trip –
something I never did, nor thought of doing.
Now
your face a chapel.
Forgive me, Mother, for all my thoughtlessness.
Forgive me, for all my silliness,
naughtiness, childishness, childlessness…
amidst my trackings, crossings, flying,
I never trekked the places you went;
your sunrises, your sunsets.

Sundial lives as bones in chapel.

## Day 3

The sun, not quite lighter than bone,
I see morning garden light outside hospice window
as you breathe slow, fairy light your palm,
knowing and not knowing this is your time
calling.
Fifty-two years of togetherness,
four hours to letting go:
twenty-three breaths a minute, then, fifteen breaths;
when you took your last, light came your way,
you gave me a beautiful death to remember you by
to show me dignity, to take stoically
four steps to breakfast on the terrace.


## Day 4

Bone china remains on the steps
inside cathedral walls.
Running my hands over ancient blue tiles,
sacred with age, with spirit, with wisdom,
I hope to hold them close
the way you kept me close
like a whale
with me inside your big, big, benevolent heart,
shielding me from evil forces,
chanting for prayers that I hurt less.
Now, your death
raked through the whale's ribcage, these pages.

## Day 5

Faith uncaged step by step from these pages
returns again and again to you, Mother.
Awhile in my pew
I watch yellow light spread around.
If only listening to you
is as easy as placing one ear
on the ivory balustrade of cloisters.
I did not know it then
that wailing within an inside is sentient.
You stopped lighting the joss incense three days
before you were called. (Did you sense?)
I leave you in a garden, burning breathless.


## Day 6

To cage and burn every page
of my unsentient days
will not bring back
your past, our past,
your pains, our grieving,
your hurts, our homelessness.
Why is it that while you stayed
We ran to live, to strive, to be anywhere but with you.
Why is it that when you left
We stay with
your absent presence?

Unscramble the catacombs of sleeping memories.

### Day 7

Cages burnt, memories buried, I wake.
Your few things (O things) – rings,
bracelets, bajus – you left behind.
Tasting your presence when
cooking plain porridge,
cutting vegetables, stirring soups,
feeling your weight
when wringing rags, clothes,
hearing your silence
when sweeping the floor, folding bedsheets.
Inside a home you left me, a blue orphanage.
Inside a bluish mosaic, space to live.


### Day 8

Awake, astir by the blues
I dream visions of you, one hundred nights,
reminding me to be prudent,
confessing death was not easy,
asking us to bring you to a doctor (finally too late),
smiling at us from afar,
calling out our names,
leaving us lost,
regretful that
we did not love you more,
more openly, more generously, more daughterly.
Head bowed, the penitent looks back.

## Day 9

From the bluest sea, first the head
of mine, rationalizing your death
as a bead in the chain of human cycle,
next your feet,
in retracing your slow, small steps,
re-wearing your kebayas,
re-arranging your photos,
re-assembling your words,
re-timing your days,
re-touching
your wrinkle of time:
those tentacular limbs reaching out.


## Day 10

Blue and black, these strapped up limbs
lost and lost, your being entrapped
between a body dying
and a soul half-wandering.
Mother, is your mind clear
with knowing unknowing,
your reasoning still lucid,
your fears founded on maternal instincts,
your worries unending,
your children never yours,
your youth, love and children:
pain or ecstasy, what's your pleasure?

### *Day 11*

Aflame in black ecstasy, orders extinguished.
How will you come home?
As azulejos, as fado
As a young carp, a beautiful maiden,
As Type A personality, entrepreneurial, progressive,
As mouse, buffalo, tiger, rabbit, dragon, snake,
As horse, goat, monkey, chicken, dog, pig,
As a fishmonger's daughter defending an immigrant lover,
As a astute mother
becoming a bodhisattva
As a black swan:
this body of lost confessions looking for the sun.

### *Day 12*

The sun orders flames in skies
Did you feel the heat of death?
Mother, you visited me last night, my last in Lisbon.
Back to me, head slightly bent, your silhouette calmed me.
You kept me in the cities I visited, the way I kept your photo
                                        in my purse.
We saw Ponte 25 Abril, the closest to the Golden Gate Bridge
I said (childlikely before) that I would bring you to. I did not.
                                        (You forgave me.)
Each street I turned, you looked out from balcony,
cooking fish in each azulejo dish,
humming a fado tune.
I want to be cleansed as heir to your music.
I yearn to weave as sardines in your oceans.

## Gold Orchid Ring Poem

I don't usually wear them
yet you bought me a gold ring.
Always thinking of the longest term;
did you already know it would be my future memory?

Shaped as an orchid flower,
its five petals your five children, your calligraphy,
you the golden course.
I now wear you to root deep, to right the swirls.

While you were in the hospice,
mixed with silent grief and eventual release,
wounded by ungrateful sons, unwise daughters,
the nation wept at our founder's passing,
aired on national tv, running on with
accolades of strength, foresight and tenacity needed
for nation-building years.

My Mother, what is strength, foresight and dignity?
As a goddess of mercy, you enlightened me*.
"This is a road we all must walk. Do not cry",
cupping my face, your ungrown child's.

You wear years of wars on your body,
scrambling over barbed wires in Syonan siege,
unladylike fights over rations, screaming hysteria, bullying…
You wear days of racial riots on your chest
as you held me, your one-year baby,
and gripped my second sis's hand
while father took a different escape route with the elder two
so that a family split might guarantee some survivors.
Before there were Scenario Planning, Risk Management,
your generation already understood crises and strategies.

You wear frugality and resourcefulness,
lived out the meaning of uncertainties before we hear of
"globalisation",
need not be taught the value of thrift, patience, resilience,
perseverance
via lessons, enrichment, training programmes or mock this and that.

Your generations had no rehearsals.

Born in a wrong decade, given few options, fewer opportunities,
misunderstood, unappreciated, unacknowledged brave females,
you are in each elderly in street corners,
your mettle underrated.

Big sis dreamt of many rows of coffins along with yours.
They are lineages of mothers, fathers, grandmothers, grandfathers,
great-grandmothers, great-grandfathers: all who went before in
centuries before;
trading blood to nourish roots of orchid trees yet to be bred
that we may be trending in futures of gold orchid rings.
You are a pure petal
present in a body yours – not yours; a country yours – not yours
(certified British Subject, given pink I/C eventually)
In a nation mine, yet to be fully fired.

*Mother passed away on the nineteenth lunar day of the second month, an
auspicious birthday of the Goddess of Mercy.*

**His Abacus**
**(for Father)**

His fingers scissored heavenly and earthly abacus beads
like a musician with his bow on stringed erhu.

His score sheet was her recital from memory on how much
fish, vegetable or fruit they sold in the morning market,
how much net earnings in coins.

He was their bookkeeper:
music to their ears were swift clicks,
harmony when both were happy with sufficiency.

Days, weeks, years polished the beads,
she was heavenly, he was earthly.
Were they a match crammed into a fixed frame?

On the inside white of a red packet,
he recorded our lunar dates and times of births,
she kept notes of vaccinations, ear-piercing days, menstruation,
                                    voice-break.

A pair as abacus seeds.
When he died
I did not think to ask why she disposed of the wooden frame.

When she died
she left me his suit of singlet and shorts she kept aside.

## Teochew Phrases

### *One Advice (with apologies to Elizabeth Bishop)*

*"A heart-throb husband is not yours to keep."*

Mother says handsome boy not your husband to keep,
pretty girl also not your wife (so wise).
Old must have money and house to keep.

Grandma feeds grandpa opium: survival trick.
Sons take and take, wives cry but still comply.
Mother says handsome boy not your husband to keep.

Marriage and children a dozen fated.
"See disguise", girls should listen to advice.
Old must have money and a house to keep.

Onion days gave way to death lines: sudden.
Rise, buy, work, sleep till dark become one sky.
Handsome boy not your husband to keep.

Good pays good, bad pays bad, time's a legend.
Fates written as ties like of pair of thighs.
Old must have money and a HDB to keep.

Heavens give what, you take what.
This life (this lie), next life, just don't ask why.
Mother says handsome boy not your husband to keep.
Old must have money and a HDB to keep.

### Down Under at Prahan Market (Established 1890) Melbourne, Australia, 2016

*"Scoop rice to barter for potato."*

At Prahan Market
I saw Singapore orchids sold at six dollars a bunch,
colourful crates of fruits and veggies priced by per kilo.
I never cared about prices back home
when I trailed behind mother for her weekly trip,
merely waited for her at our regular beehoon stall,
eating my standard plate with fishcake
as she chatted cheerfully with each owner.

Mother was the real businesswoman
handling research in the purest fashion.

Her sharp math, crisp gossip
straight from the wok like deep fried you tiao,
her updated price list from perishables to property
all in her head
while mine was a sieve.

Unschooled
she mastered more than I could.

### *Your Teochew Proverbs*

Now that you passed,
your proverbs ring pure and clear:


Paper cannot wrap fire.

What is yours is yours.

To be old is difficult, counting on children even more so.

A tiger's legacy: it's skin.
A man's: his name.

A flower does not bloom forever.
The sky is not forever fine.

The rich can be poor, the poor can be rich.

Fire and water have no kin.

People act, heavens watch.


And now, I miss your voice,
forgetting my Teochew words.
How mute have I become,
when earlier, how deaf.

## Is it Love?

### (i) *Crush*

That which you proffered
I kept in a shoebox at the far corner in the
bottomest drawer of my hand-me-down wardrobe.

That I saw again when packing
overgrown and outdated clothes
as recyclables for community projects.

At a gathering of old friends
as you shook my hand, held it –
I shudder at the violence I might have dealt you.

## (ii) *Decades Later*

Decades later
when we met at your child's ballet audition,
you confessed to me
that it was my bashful quiet which struck you:
how I would be at the canteen corner drinking only coffee,
unfailing each school morning.

Decades later
I am now the one struck by your openness,
Perhaps it needed a divorce and a sense of lost chance
to share your crush,
so normal, so special
so muted now.

Decades ago
I would not know how to admit to you, or others
why I sit alone mostly at recess was that
my pocket money could only afford a black coffee,
so crucial to budget for lunch later.

Far from bashful was I.
Hunger shapes love.

### (iii) *Arrival and Departure*

For you, a river
for you, a rainfall

while
I am no angry woman
I'm no pining lover,
no fallen maiden,
no seduced lover,
no seraphina,
I howl dialectal.

What's this age we live in?
In this land of virtual highways,
what of hills and vales?

If I stare long enough,
listen deep enough
will I become water,
be awash with wisdom and tender power,
might I run to a river or a harbour?

I shadow your footsteps
1000 lines away.

## (iv) *Leaving*

so you see my smile
what of my ache?

so you hold my hand
what of my ache?

so you wrap my waist
what of my ache?

so you kiss my lips
what of my space?

so you ring me around
what of my dreams?

At the end of a loving tenderness,
moist shadows mourn.

How might I use dead white man's words
to sing a yellow-skin woman's grief?

## (v) *An Ache*

Is an ache a wave
crashing as a surf on a shore?
So close my hand trembles
when I feel the crest at times retreating
at the loss of my sighting.

Some days
I feel as a boat on windy waters
to berth at a nameless harbour, nameless city,
a hull needing repair,
with tiny leaks I slow sail.

Some days
I am a ball stuck in a wire netting
at the fenced up basket-ball court.
All I need is a tug,
and my tears come free.

After the ache,
days go on, must go on.
Leaving me to kiss shadows
of moonless nights.

## My Wallpaper

### (i) *Having Fun*

One morning she wakes up
hearing strange sounds:

Chinese mee is identity,
lala is shellfish in her la la land,
ports of call become cooking pots,
khaki colour becomes a friendly kaki.

Speciality misheard as special tea,
when hungry I imagine
my love is a red, red roast.
french fries is fresh rice
stomach is Starbucks.

During PSLE
my worried mother
fed me chicken brain
instead
I became chicken feed.
Do I become a small shrub
when birds and humans
shit close by
to fertilize my growth?

## (ii) *Insufficient*

How different is a river view
from a view of a river?
surely different to views of a river or river a view?

Since we do not,
as the philosopher claims,
step into the same river twice,
do we likewise not read the same sentence twice?

Might it be possible for a past and present to both be in a same river,
its future too, at any one minute?

Or in another minute, its past present future would have changed?

What remains is "syntax is insufficient for semantics".
And how do I say all of this in Teochew?

Should I compare me to a monsoon rain?
Dare I borrow Dante's mezzo del cammin?

Are fairies "xian nu"?
What's the word in Malay for it?

## (iii) *Digits*

We can solve inequality using Mathematics,
using no calculator, only digits
if there's a formula.

We may substitute, substract,
add, divide, multiply;
values, functions all clarify.
Everything to the power of n is contained within a page.

Can we solve inequality in life,
needing no formula when there's a God?
We are not only digits.

We may supply welfare, add a human touch,
divide the pain, multiply means.
Values, functions pacify.
Everything to the power of n is no longer contained.

Is much of Mathematics symbolic language?
Is much of life symbolic?
How much of digital life is life?

## (iv) *Plot Farming*

Geographically,
latitude and longitude
define our dot on a world map;

a dot since we have little land expanse,
so we re-shape our coastlines
to reclaim a plot historically

a plot that was once a tropical plantation
which made way for MNC plants, mrt stations,
now planting futures in smart city digitalisation.

Economists and planners sow digital fertilizers of unknown yields.
Are we encouraged to be farmers of intellectual crops?
Would poetry farming be sustainable?

## (v) *The Lord is my shepherd, I shall not want. Psalm 23:1*

Add to cart: I click,
swipe, tap, click: add to cart.
A paradise gained online
when there are voluminous choices;
when vendors offered options, stressors,
lost in my mind's paradise,
is my hand a dragnet in a wild wide web?

My cart gains items,
I gain weight,
my head burdens,
I own more of everything except
certainty and space;
I lose currency
with God.

From my deep dark web,
I flounder,
gasping,
The Lord is my shepherd,
I shall not want,
seeking my lost paradise
where five loaves and two fish suffice.

# A Soldier's Song, a Civilian's Echo

## (i) *Colour of Cholera*

*The Changi Emblem at the entrance to Changi Museum – a charcoal etching entitled "Two Malarias and a Cholera" by Ray Parkins.*

So you told them
of our lives,
now etched emblematic
as charcoal art
on an island small
(insular while international.)

Would I guess
our black white skeletons
hovering between life and death
on the Thai-Burma Railway

would make it across
to this end,
while living a past –
black white lines like
black white history in
newsprint and textbooks
once upon a time

now sketched in the spaces between
lines, curves, on pillars and walls
of a small museum?

Our backs to you,
how do you see my choking within
tasting so the cords of blood
singing hymns of life
while dying.

## (ii) *Size of "The Slab"*

*In the middle of a Changi cell is a 18-inch-wide concrete "bed". Inside each cell, a lavatory made it one with the most modern amenity.*

footstepsstirmefromconcrete
bedrelivingalostworldbehind
dooralavatoryisheaveninhell

## (iii) *Changi Fairies*

*The Changi Quilts were initiated by Ethel Mulvanery, a Canadian internee. There are now three surviving quilts, the British Quilt, the Australian Quilt and the Japanese Quilt.*

My finger dances on your soft square
when you arrive
I know my beloved is mine
and I am hers.

I was wrong to think women weak
I was wrong to think men strong
I was wrong to think victors clear-headed
I was wrong to think prisoners weak-willed.

I was wrong to think sewing sissy
and I would be more wrong to think
my own stitches could patch my tear-ed body
as swiftly,
neatly,
surely
as your needlework.

Small squares make loving largess.

oh my beloved is here
oh my Changi fairy dear.

## (iv) *Artistes*

*Angela Bateman was a 60-year-old artist interned at Changi Gaol and Sime Road Camp. Two additional paintings were found hidden on the back of two of her art works when the latter were sent for restoration upon being acquired by the Changi Museum.*

You in our midst of wailing walls,
silent sinking nights
are wise enough,
behind grilled windows,
to seal future life
on canvas.

On the back of one sheet
you budget
another drawing,
another day expanding
like a child growing hope

so that
we may be safe
in your framed resthouse
not at Sime Road Camp,

but at 1000 Changi North Road.

## (v) *Grieving Artfully*

*Bombardier Stanley Warren was tasked to paint the walls of the chapel at Robert Barracks.*

My brother,
you are a light 38 kilogramme frame
colouring the concrete walls of St Luke's Chapel
with your pains.

Yours is a
grief
of quiet art
while we try to help with rough haste
by stealing the billiards-chalk blue,
battleship grey lorry paints
that you may colour our greying daze,
offering our human hair as your brush.

Luke is with you,
with us,
with the past,
with the present,
with the future
forever and evermore
amen.

## (vi) *Chapel Cross*

*There is a brass cross in a glass box on the altar of the open-air Changi Chapel. It was crafted from scraps of brass, its base part of a used 4.5-inch howitzer (artillery) shell. Designed by Reverend Eric Cordingly and made by Staff Sergent Harry Stogden – both POWS – the cross was taken by Rev Cordingly to the Thai-Burma Railway, back to Changi and then to England. Harry Stogden survived the war but died of beri-beri on board a hospital ship homeward bound from Japan. In 2001, Rev Cordingly's family returned the cross to Changi, and Stogden's son was given the honour of placing the cross in its present position.*

Today
through my sunnies,
I hear gory glory
of Singapore's first airfield sealed with POWs' blood-sweat;
of savage nobility
alive on Death Railway;
of life in a postcard
between internees and those outside,
of a wide world concealed
in a matchbox radio;
of cold comforts
consisting of a cigarette;
listening to Changi AIF Concerts' Party;
"Of thoughts far away" in historical time
pulsating in present,
current "Sights o' Changi".

Today I hum unheard songs of
soldiers deep asleep
to make meek memory
awake,
absent pain
quicken
in open-air pews

so that like you;
imagining Reverend Cordingly
speak of your father's faith
in bearing his cross,
crafting it from brass and artillery shell,
freed finally off the waters of Nagasaki;
like you,
lost son of his emplacing present position
the original cross here in Changi,
you make peace with man's original sin.
I too,
still daughter of island small,
make peace with secular sins.

Although not a soldier fit for fighting,
I am civilian internee
adrift on seas of cash, credit cards, career,
condominium, club membership;
wondering when Changi colours,
communities, countries will converge
to berth on island small.

## My City, My Sayang

How is my city a song?
How do I float tunes in her river?
Do I go whistling in her gardens,
swinging between her chic skyscrapers?

I want to feel the jingle in her steps,
I want to touch the twinkle in her clap,
I want to slurp her moon as icy pop,
to wear her sundrop as a ring.

I want to be attuned to her river.
hear centuries in her wayang,
glide with her grace to embrace
my city, my sayang.

To those who raised me on do re mi, 123;
to those whose songs I hear and sing;
to those whose tunes are not yet heard;
I want to court them, pitch them, harmonise their melodies.

How is my city a song?
Hear her from within.

## Sun-Skink Lizard's Blues

I bask in sundried leaf litter,
skinny dip in monsoon mulch.
Ferns tickle, shrubs comfort, grass shelter.
Sometimes I hear near my sky
footsteps crushing parched understorey,
at times, a palm brushing an ant off a ankle,
my eyes hold hungry on my blue babe
(like a wide-eyed adam on his eve).
We are all territorial in our rainforest hearth.
They sometimes think me thoughtless,
call their enemies lizard brains,
driven by desires and desires,
clueless as accomplices.

They do not glide from trunk to trunk,
they do not eat fresh produce,
my daily diet of flies, ants, beetles
is organic brain food, superfuel for body engines.
Do they hear thunder before calm?
Or see rainbows in spaces between sun rays?
Or taste sweet spots of time* in a faraway forest?
Can they speed steady up on Meranti's body?
I hear them in crazy cars outside my habitat.

I look one in the glassy eye,
a second, an eternity:
a finger clicks a snap, kisses a screen,
in an instant, I die as a naturalist**.
I glide up further into main canopy to receive sky,
my body falls like rain that falls and falls
to seep deep and deep into primordial soil,
relive a little in rainforest heart
to grow as another lizard
as ants walk by,
to live a little.

*Allusion to a line in William Wordsworth's "The Prelude" (1805).
**Allusion to Seamus Heaney's "Death of a Naturalist" (1966).

## Simply Being Garden
### (SBG aka Singapore Botanic Garden)

Once upon a time was a sapling spirited
from Fort Canning to Whampoa's Tanglin,
from garden plot to experimental crop,
spice spot to orchard plot;
a flowering tree from a first seed.

Here leaf litter encircles trees, echoing earth;
carpeting in green brown grounds, softening footfalls,
offering kisses between spaces, between raindrops.
At core, a six-hectare primary forest –
house of tigers from centuries before.

In early years were scattered sepiaed parchment of
mismanagement, debts, zoo animals within,
made way for colonial landscape on garden's fate
until Mad Ridley sowed his herring-bone success,
reaping regional riches through rubber's conquest.

Now, Vanda Miss Joaquim hosts leaders and future fame,
today's hybrid was yesterday's child, tomorrow's parent,
welcoming, welcoming
citizens, visitors, immigrants, maids, dogs and joggers,
passing through at different gates and times,
presently.

Men created swan lake, cornered monkeys collected specimens.
Post-war trials starved pre-war vibrancy.
Simply, garden turned breeding bed for diversity.
Independent intensive tree planting
grew public park into picnic-baskets.
Dreaming couples, parents, children, graduands stream in
like epiphytes, terrestrials, climbers, like stamens and stigmas,

like bees, birds, beetles, butterflies,
all creatures great and small, giant or slight, light or dark
like a Noah's ark in a city park.

Presented as a nursery of living future,
programmed as a library of foliaged past,
heritage trees root sturdy next to sculptures,
children on green hearth learn to evolve fast,
understanding how saplings incubate,
needing nourishment to pulsate,
enduring elements from nature's flow,
savouring blossoms in a rosette of leaves,
catching raindrops as rainbows,
organizing scents as perfumed glows.

## among all
## (ICA, Lavender Street, 2018)

would there be digits flashing electric
by which to trace forms? it might have been un-
heard of like an unseen bomb, save by the Lord
far away&long ago in archipelagos.

it was different at colonial office
of a time and clime where dialogue dialects
were not antilanguage politics,
where houses were nests, and birds connect.

would the sunlight which shone on coolies then
sink the same heat into present refugees?
Is it by nature that we move from plight
to fight – a sequence with contingencies?

wander among all as a spirit i do.
would our numbers, if tracked, have been untrue?

*Base text words from "would it have been" by Arthur Yap:*
*would, it, bomb, &, different, of, antilanguage, were, sunlight, into, by,*
*sequence, all, untrue.*

**Still Life**

**(i)** *Market Stall*

Old bald man at market yong tau foo store
stands below his sign:
10 pieces for $4, $2 per bowl, 50 cents rice.

In between serving customers
before the weekend crowd builds up,
one hand on waist, the other holding a glass,
he sips kopi c,
eating his own home-made fried bean curd
stuffed with filling,
clearly food-tasting and hunger-stalling
while his wife munches her rice-kueh hastily,
preparing bowls of mee hoon yong tau hoo expertly.
(talk about multi-tasking).

For just one brief moment,
they sit down on the plastic bench in front of their store,
within my earshot,
they discuss last night's ma-piew pou*
(we all have our strike-rich dreams).

As if on cue,
several customers appear in a queue.
Old man darts back in front of his steaming pot,
old woman stands by his side to pass him the ready-to-be-served
                                                    bowls
awaiting an experienced ladle,
while another elderly kin is inside laying out more slices.

* *horse-racing tabloid*

## (ii) *Trolley Pushing*

A middle-aged karung guni man
pushes a trolley of discarded boxes,
empty egg cartons, cardboard slabs, et cetera
across a school compound,
unaware a patient car trails behind.

A young man pushing his trolley of wares
shouts him a warning in Hokkien.

Karung guni man turns to check his fate,
swerves skilfully to the side of the road,
smiles at the young chap
who offers him a cheeky deal:
"sell you want or not. 50 cents"

As the car drives past him, past the security guard post,
the two exchange looks of brotherhood.

On their return from the big rubbish dump,
the young chap lets his empty trolley
roll down the slight slope,
whistling a cheery tune,
light-hearted after the unloading.

The karung guni man holds his empty trolley by one hand
as he walks in a different direction,
while another elderly man with a light limp
pushes a market cart
as his steady walking stick.

### (iii) *Roadside Cleaner*

He is bent
as he pushes the trolley
with black plastic dustbin,
with a broom and dustpan
hung at one side.

His right palm grips the handle
almost as if it is for support.

He is a skeleton inside the baggy blue uniform.

A strong wind from somewhere
destabilises him,
the plastic bag keels over to let defiant litter
disperse as chaotic rioters.

How does his daily battles with the elements
compare with my office politics?

Calmly he picks up the truant trash
with a pair of tongs,
unaware of my witness
from a bistro so near
yet so faraway.

## (iv) *At a Café*

Red checked shirt, short sleeves, black pants,
red waist-apron uniform he wears,
stacking porcelain mugs to fill a tray.
He focuses on arranging them,
swiftness his pattern, packing each to optimise space.

When he comes round to my table a second time,
eyes as if asking if I minded
I say "thank you",
he almost drops the mug.

At another table,
elbows on it, a man's palm encircles a mug of hot drink,
thumbs twirling,
leaning back onto a plastic chair to watch the traffic go by,

just like that
while a harried crowd
walks past him without a second glance.

Is he on leave or jobless?

## (v) *Schoolgirls*

Four schoolgirls in uniform sharing a meal:
half a baguette, a bowl of corn soup, a baked potato with
bacon bits and a peach tart:
comforting tableau at Delifrance,
with the sound system
crooning American pop songs.

Do they dream of rajas and princesses
afloat on their luxury cruise liners, velvety couches,
day-bed fly-netted?
Or of boys and dudes, lavish or romantic dates?
Or of bags and accessories?
Or of grades and trophies?
Or… or … or…

What's a schoolgirl's dreams made of these days?

### (vi) *Child Playing at Water Fountain*
### *(Bugis Junction, Singapore)*

At a fountain near a shopping mall:
a blonde mother looks on as her toddler boy sits
at the edge of a wet circle,
points at the spouts,
giggling when water squirts out.
(His fingers make magic.)
Bolder, he goes nearer the lowest spurt,
places his palm for a point of contact
to give it a tickle.
He dances with the fountain, thoroughly soaked,
thoroughly drenched, thoroughly happy.

A grandparently pair guard a grandson:
grandpa holding onto him with a leash,
grandma sees the boy reaching out to grasp at water,
she scoops him up and brings him close to spurting spring,
the squiggling boy grabbing at water,
the grandma grabbing him safe,
the grandpa standing by ready.

## (vii) *Scene at Yakun Coffee Shop*

"Mei mei, you want cake?"

A grandma asks her grandchildren who are on school break.
"One milo peng" for the two girls, and a kopi c for herself.
They share their grandma's kaya toast too, picking at
                                        the bread cubes,
not talking or looking much at her, eyes glued onto mobile screens.
She sits silent looking at them.

Does she wonder how many years are left of her grandbaby-sitting
responsibilities for her working child's sake?

## (viii) *City Moments*

(a)
I want to grow old with beauty,
will I snub the cosmetic scapel?
listen to the wisdom of wrinkle?
wear the sky as a sarong,
and walk barefoot with elegance?

How would you grant me that
where tarred roads can cut me,
where crushed soles seem common
from elevator use, traffic accidents,
politics and neuroses?

(b)
These days we are not told
to go and catch a falling star
but to go and catch a bargain
on Single's Day, Black Friday … what have you.
*Add to card*

These days we are not told
to make much of our virgin days
to gather rosebuds whenever, whatever, however
but download apps, more apps, and still more apps.
*Add to cart*
*Add to cut*

(c)

Rain smacking hot tarred roads
looks like black-star snowflakes.

Silvery water lines on grey land is
artful rain.

Bubbles near a growing puddle
become slivers of water, then ponds, then rivers, then...

Colourful umbrellas accompany swift feet,
burdened mothers shield prams assiduously.

One lady spreads open a shawl
as she heads into the rains.

To watch the rains fall we don't do anymore
when our eyes are distracted with devices of other skies.

Lines from the swift end of a canopy screen roof
are twinkling stars as they kiss the road light.

### (ix) *Outside the Theatre*

Before the famed performance
theatre ushers wait.

On their black/white uniform lapels
gold name tags,

jobscope artfully crammed within a frame,
milling over logistics, they act.

Inside lights are dimmed,
outside, artful life lives on.

## (x) *Opera@work*

Masks: surgical, cloth, painted,
stylised gestures, kabuki-like,
mannequined exits and entrances,
precision-timed
to be seen by
the right people at the right second at the right place:
shrewd staging.

When deputised with power,
one might consolidate
with blatant bias:
sure proof way of demi-god cape,
surely
a wolf within.

## Looking at Stalls Under Tree by Fullerton Building
### (Undated watercolour painting by Lim Cheng Hoe)

They are a pair on canvas:
one alive with shifting light;
warm sepia of a late afternoon,
the other a still life of bricks
brushed on as background; in plein air.

There are three dustbins at the bottom right,
next to a no-parking sign, discreet pride,
with adjacent shophouses
(now refurbished as eateries and bistros)
while a patch of foliaged green at the
far top left fans shade to the stall vendors.

I imagine

They would know each other,
they would look at each other's
carts, bowls, goods,
their various wares.
Same spot, same time.
Monsoon or sunshine,
dark or light.

They must learn a little of each
beginning:
what clan, what village, what province, what household,
kin, siblings, extended family…
parallel plots of fleeing wars, finding promises of rainbows,
each day a little sharing under shaded tents,
a staple like the food and goods they hawk.

The concrete Fullerton rightly situated as backdrop,
with human figures
in red, blue or yellow
centred by your light,
green at top left, bins at bottom right,
you frame fluidly
a stoicity.

## Singapore River, 1962
## (Painting by Lim Cheng Hoe)

Why do you blow her surface with colours? (what of her
                                    cruising insides?)
Which are your pains? (How do the bruising bumboats sway you?
Who are those you reach to hold? Do you quiver with their sighs?
From land, you trace slivers of living in broad rivers and streams.
For perspective: crossing curves and lines at far ends on canvas;
lively orange roof-cover of foregrounded sampan and working
                                    men as bent, brushed blobs;
blues diluted, greys calm, birds, creatures, fish near muddy water edge
with a faint but clean wood-stick to guide our eye on this water level
furthering its history onto the lined buildings and warehouses at
                                    the other end,
conquerors and merchants alike,
This is no river of Babylon. You do not weep there.
It is an ancient river of pleasures and pains. It's sungei, 河 and nati.
A river is a river by any name, do the drops agree with each other
                                    like passing souls?
She who moves, murmurs, shivers, whirs; whooshing, splashing,
                                    wishing, singing, buried within.
On land, are you catching currents? Do you measure ocean drops
                                    with breath-stroke?
Do I measure your brush strokes? Do you feel that all rivers run
                                    into the sea? How might I keep
current with you? She gathering you, you gliding over to me,
                                    all of us still voyaging on a riverbed,
asleep and awake.

**Restoration**
**(Gallery 3, National Art Gallery –**
**Imagining Country and Self)**


Of the fourteen frames on the beautiful Indies,*
one shades an inside view: "A lazy afternoon".**
Country, self, a past with buildings dance daring.
History shapes an exterior interior.

Now offices and judiciary stand
connected to past civics; present art.
Neo classical renamed modernity,
"Siapa nama saya?" claims reality.

Twin limbs rise as architectural feats,
one swings supreme courtly, one hauls a city.
Both held in sync on internal bridges,
gesturing, advancing, sashaying

via entrance veil, swirling on rotunda,
anointing presence on green Padang.


* *Paintings in the Dutch tradition of Mooi Indie (the beautiful Indies).*
** *Title of the 1859 oil on canvas by Jan Daniel Beynon (b 1830,*
*d 1877).*

## Retention – Mui Tsai, Visitor and Chief Justice (Chief Justice's Chamber)

"Before law and land, I swear justice right."
Inside a foundation stone, as retention – a time capsule.
"Big person*, mui tsai small, no right to fight".

Thieves, killers stood in dock, feeling contrite?
In year 3000, as history, straits coins teach currency.
"Before land and law, I use private lift as a right."

Girl slavery – when did they come to light?
In year 2017, capsuled coins become bitcoins.
"Big man, mui tsai's half-closed eyes see night light."

Order, black and white, square patterns bright.
Earth and Heaven constitute foundation of life.
"I swear justice before land and law rights."

In some households, men ate food and fresh girls.
Do crimes within meet justice without?
"Big man, mui tsai go quiet with no light."**

Thieves, killers, predators now meet law quite
differently; digital is earth-heaven.
With land and law, justice serves in full light.
Mui tsai could not rage into her good night.**

* *Big person – literal translation from Chinese, a term of address for a judge, a magistrate or a master.*
** *Allusion to Dylan Thomas' "Do not go gentle into the good night".*

## What a Silkworm Heard

*Inspired by the Silk Princess, a Chinese wood panel painting from the 7th and 8th century. The BBC's "A History of the World" describes the artefact: "According to this legend, a Chinese princess smuggled the secret of how to make silk out of China and into the country of her new husband, the king of Khotan. As she was a princess the border guards did not dare search her. In this painting her elaborate headdress conceals the cocoon of the silk moth and the seeds of the mulberry tree."*


You are an escort in my headdress
which everyone claims beautiful;
(they do not see it heavy on my head)
I smuggle you into Khotan land
that I might remember home.

How would they know
I feel giddy in a swaying sedan?
(What is it like to walk on land?)

How would they know
being carried everywhere is tiresome?
How would they know
I am angry at such arrangements?

I smile to be filial or pious.
What is land?
In my husband's kingdom,
will they see my headdress as beautiful?
will they see me soft?

In my days,
I keep mute

to be beautiful
still
to be beautiful
weak
to be beautiful
soft
to be beautiful
half full
to be beautiful
half awake
to be beautiful
all beautiful to be needed
all of soft silk
route
to my future fame
framed in a silk screen painting
perhaps
that I may remain
eternally beautifully
mute,
virtually real.

## Travelling Lines

### *At Lhasa*
### *(Potala Palace, Tibet, 2000)*

On the steps of Potala Palace
I watched a young backpacker couple pose on the Square
and then kiss with no inhibition, arms encircling each other.

Do the red-robed monks see and think of such encircling
as they circle their prayer-wheels?
Perhaps they transcend as they meditate.

### *Swat Valley*
### *(Pakistan, 2006)*

A common sight on the Karakorum Highway is children at
the edge of the curvy road holding out cherries, reddened and
deepened against white plates. At Swat Valley, the children
hold out plastic bags with ripened plums for us to inspect, then
(hopefully) buy.

Committees of men gather around rickshaws or squat on
rooftops, inside is Sufi beauty, outside harsh rockfalls.

Toilet is one with a view because out in the open, there's only four
slabs of metal to make up a cubicle. Pantheon of ancient gods,
city gods, where are you?

### Busker Guitarist
### (Cambridge, UK, 2010)

The electronic guitarist busking in front of the Great St Mary's
Church strumming cheerily to no one in particular. (Does he
believe God hears?)

Only a stand-alone boy listening intently while three other adult
tourists lick their ice-cream cones with their backs to the busker
for the view towards the Colleges look greener.

This is my tableau of summer time in postcard Cambridge.

The busker pauses to reach for his mobile. The sky remains still.


### A Donkey's Journey
### (Oia, Santorini, 2014)

Wearing his ringing collar, he gives his owner the means to
transport food every 10 minutes. He climbs up cobbled cliffways
to deliver mineral water, boxes of fresh produce to a restaurant
famed for its terraced views of Oia sunset.

Tourists from packed coaches come out at a precise time to order
a set menu offered at a special price so that they might sit sunsetly
to sigh at hues.

Do colours in real life cost more for its transience?

## A List from my Santorini Guide

On the island there is no traffic light, only fifty-five taxis serving
the touristy isle, all Mercedes. Fifty thousand cruise liners this
summer, a drop, the country is in debt. Once named "strongyli",
a volcanic eruption shaped her differently. White houses with blue
domes disguised its flag-flying colours as a protest under Turkish
occupation. There are four hundred churches due to fears, status
and pragmatics, her true name is Thira but Venetians called her
Santorini. Her vineyards are shrubs. Profiti Alias is her monastery
at the highest spot, also a military base. Monks claim they are
roasted literally. Forty-five years ago, Santorini only had cherry
tomatoes and grapes, now hordes of savage tourists breed in the
summer. For a princely tag, I am transported to a cave dug out to
make a blue dream home, and so I dream my dream in a blue,
blue cave.

## Slow Mail to Cavafy
### (Athens, 2014)

Since I cannot really make my life as I want (as you advised), I
strive for this (for once) to be as slow as I can. I will not degrade it
through associating too much with virtuality, through texting and
social-webbing. I'll try not to be a bothersome stranger (as you
named it); sail instead for my Ithaca (as you wisely reminded me),
knowing too well, only water matters.

### Spring in a Liveable City
### (Down Under, 2016)

Along a city's famous streets, a glass panel with Arial bold letters
advertises "For lease, creative office space". Next to it, a homeless
woman with a blanket rag spread as ground sheet on concrete
makes a home, just underneath the invite "To rent".

At another laneway, a man covers himself with a large brown
cardboard. Equally nonchalant are tourists and residents. A rare
sideway glance from a passerby. The driver on his mobile cleaning
up vehicle turns his steering wheel to sidestep the sleeping man,
considerate gesture in one of the world's liveable cities.


### Days at a Rainforest Lodge
### (Peru, 2018)

*(i) Boys Repairing Boats*
*(December afternoon, Corto Maltes)*

They are young, tanned and wizened.

The boat roof leaked after pouring rains.
They rip off the top canvas layer,
staple on a new piece:
one stretches out the sheet, neat and taut like his muscles,
the other uses a heavy-duty stapler to tag the long panel to
wooden boat roof frame.

When one end is finished, seemingly pleased
they take turns to gulp from an orange Gatorade.

The winds take a sudden gust, the pair wrestles it with co-
ordination and muscle manoeuvring.

When the job is finally done,
one of them climbs onto the roof,
lies flat as on a clean bed, arms spread wide.
He whistles and calls out to the girlish kitchen hand
who dangles her legs at a log-bench near the jetty,
ear phones plugged into a mobile.

When she finally looks up and sees him hail her,
she shakes her head, returns to her music, shy,
head turns upwards to the Amazonian sky.


*(ii) Watch Rains*

I watch the rain from the shelter of a thatched roof porch
overlooking Madre de Dios,
drops draining away from eaves.

A Greek mother-daughter pair sit silent in company;
one finishing her cigarette,
the other scribbling on a page.

A Turkish old couple,
also quiet, also smoking,
with empty wine glasses on their deck tables.

Out at the jetty which the lodge staff call the port,
one of the workhands caught a rodent
and offers it to the boatman as a pet.

Each of us waiting for the rains to stop
before our first guided rainforest walk,
patience ahead of us.

# Pottering with Words

## (i) *Words are Needles*

Words are needles touching vinyl
circling in my head.
I am a broken instrument in need of repair.

No one remakes radios or record-players,
so little need now with i-pods and i-tunes.
An expert mechanic is a rare good.

Who cares about a shepherd living quiet
on a hill called Gethsamene?
No GPS could locate him.

## (ii) *Words are Wafers*

I leap off the eaves of a pagoda drawn on rice paper,
balance on stilts,
I let you dance on me as a mythical qilin.

Words are wafers on my lips,
my blood your red wine,
my heart is cold with ghosts.

Should I stare long enough
at the road in front,
will it become a Hiroshige wave?

I hear Virginia's screams,
see Sylvia's genius buried with Ted's letters,
little know of Vivienne's incarceration.

Her wasteland untreated by Eliot,
As she proffered him his fame,
he stood safe, she stays insane.

## (iii) *Touching Hart*
## *(Reading some Hart Crane)*

When you found me,
I carried a dead body around.
It cast no shadow in the day,
did not wake like a vampire on full moon
or feed on another's blood.

Was that how you felt in those maniac
thousand words lying in your isle of Carib?
Drunk sober: was your price of genius
floating as a magician on waves of madness?

Tonight,
Hart, with you, I sink,
not over Brooklyn Bridge,
having crossed it once,

tonight I dived in.

Is this how you feel, Hart,
in a long, long night
longing, lingering.
who's to say it's a hand or a body writing?

Who's to say, who's to say?

Hart, why did you sleep in your river deep
to drown and to float?

## (iv) *Small Bites*

A poem is a tray of dim sum.

Ingredients being minced meat, chives.
minced words, prawns, scallops,
greased grief, crunchy pork ribs, chicken feet,
anger, hurts, siew mai,
hostility, envy
wrapped with homemade beancurd skins;
memories folded neatly
into chee cheong fun or spring rolls,
sometimes baked as radish cake,
at times steamed as char siew pau,
shaped like us, meat with outer wrap:
consumable.

## (v) *Stitching*

Is a manuscript a season fashion show?
Words sewn together for fall, spring, summer and winter.
What about monsoon and tropical seasons?

Fashion wears words or is it vice versa?
Couture is expensive erotica?
See-through material sheer provocative art?

Stitching is spatial, writing reciprocal.
Language making as messy as the fragments of assorted material
scattered on the maker's floor.

## COMMISSIONED POEMS

"Restoration" and "Retention" were commissioned by Singapore Writers Festival 2017 published in *Eye/Feel/Write* (Squircle Line Press, 2017).
"My City, My Sayang" was commissioned by Singapore Teacher's Academy for the aRts (STAR), Ministry of Education (2017).
"District 1: Tew Chew Street (1930s)" was commissioned by Poetry Festival Singapore 2019 and published in *Contour: A lyric cartography of Singapore* (Ethos Books, 2019).
"among all" was commissioned by Desmond Kon and published in *Seven Hundred Lines, a crown of found/fount sonnets* (Squircle Line Press, 2019).
"Simply Being Garden" and "Sun-skin Liazard's Blues" were commissioned by Singapore Botanic Garden and published in *Nature of Poetry* (National Parks Board, 2019).
"Looking at Stalls Under Tree by Fullerton Building" and "Singapore River, 1962 (Painting by Lim Cheng Hoe)" were commissioned by National Gallery Singapore in 2019.

## PREVIOUSLY PUBLISHED POEMS

"Gold Orchid Ring" in *Written Country: The History of Singapore through Literature* (Landmark Books, 2016).
The sequence "A soldier's song, a civilian's echo" in *Sound of Mind* (Ethos Books, 2016).
The sequence "Simple days" in *Lost Bodies: Poems between Singapore and Portugal* (Ethos Books, 2016).
"What a Silkworm Heard" in https://iwp.uiowa.edu/silkroutes.

## ABOUT THE POET

Heng Siok Tian has written six collections of poetry: *Crossing the Chopsticks and Other Poems* (1993), *My City, My Canvas* (1999), *Contouring* (2004), *Is my body a myth* (2011), *Mixing Tongues* (2011), and *Grandma's Attic, Mom's HDB, My Wallpaper* (2021). Her poems have been anthologised in numerous books.

A Fellow of the Iowa International Writing Program (2000) on a National Arts Council Fellowship, she has participated in literary events in China, USA, Philippines, Stockholm, Sweden and France.

She is on the selection panel of the Creative Arts Programme and is a Facilitator and Mentor from 1991 to the present, for which she was given the Distinguished CAPer and Outstanding Mentor awards by the Gifted Education Branch of the Ministry of Education, Singapore in 2001 and 2009 respectively. A teacher by profession, Siok Tian was given the National Day Long Service Award in 2015.